Dhuwa ŋarra yurru bukuwikama ŋan̲d̲i'mirriŋuna man̲d̲any ŋarraku. Dr Barbara Laklak Burarrwaŋa-Ganambarr ga Ruthie l̲ul̲'warriwuy Ganambarr. Dhiyaku djorrawu ŋarra wukirri man̲d̲akalaŋuwuy.

I would like to dedicate this book to my mother Dr Barbara Laklak Burarrwaŋa-Ganambarr and her sister Ruthie l̲ul̲'warriwuy Ganambarr. To my mother who planted the seed of knowledge in my mind and nurtured it.

About the Indigenous Literacy Foundation

The Indigenous Literacy Foundation (ILF) is a national charity working with Aboriginal and Torres Strait Islander remote Communities across Australia.
We are Community-led, responding to requests from remote Communities for culturally relevant books, including early learning board books, resources, and programs to support Communities to create and publish their stories in languages of their choice.

In 2024 the ILF won the Astrid Lindgren Memorial Award, given annually to a person or organisation for their outstanding contribution to children's or young adult literature.

First published in 2025 by the
Indigenous Literacy Foundation
Gadigal Country
Level 17/207 Kent Street Sydney NSW 2000
ilf.org.au

Cataloguing-in-Publication details are available from the National Library of Australia
www.trove.nla.gov.au

ISBN 9781923179608

Typesetting and design by Lee Burgemeestre
Printed in China by RR Donnelley Asia Printing Solutions Limited

Ŋäṉḏi ga Gatapaŋa

Mum and the Buffalo

A Story by
Djawundil Maymuru
(Djawundilwuŋu Dhäwu)

Illustrated by children at Yirrkala School

Djawundil

Nhämirri bukmak, ŋarraya yäku Djawundil. Ŋarraya yurru dhäwu nhumaŋgu l̲akama Ŋän̲d̲iwalaŋuwuy ga nhanŋu yapa'mirriŋu Ruthie.

Hello everyone, my name is Djawundil. I am going to tell you a story about my mother and her sister Ruthie.

Ruthie
Mum

Waŋganythu waluyu man̲d̲a nhina bala waŋganhamina gungawu gulkthunawu. Ŋayi Ŋän̲d̲iwuya wuŋgan yäku Roger ga yindi ŋayi ŋunhiyi wuŋgantja djäl malthunawu gurrut̲umiwu wayaŋgu.

One morning they were planning to go out and collect pandanus. Mum had a dog named Roger who loved going out with the family.

Roger

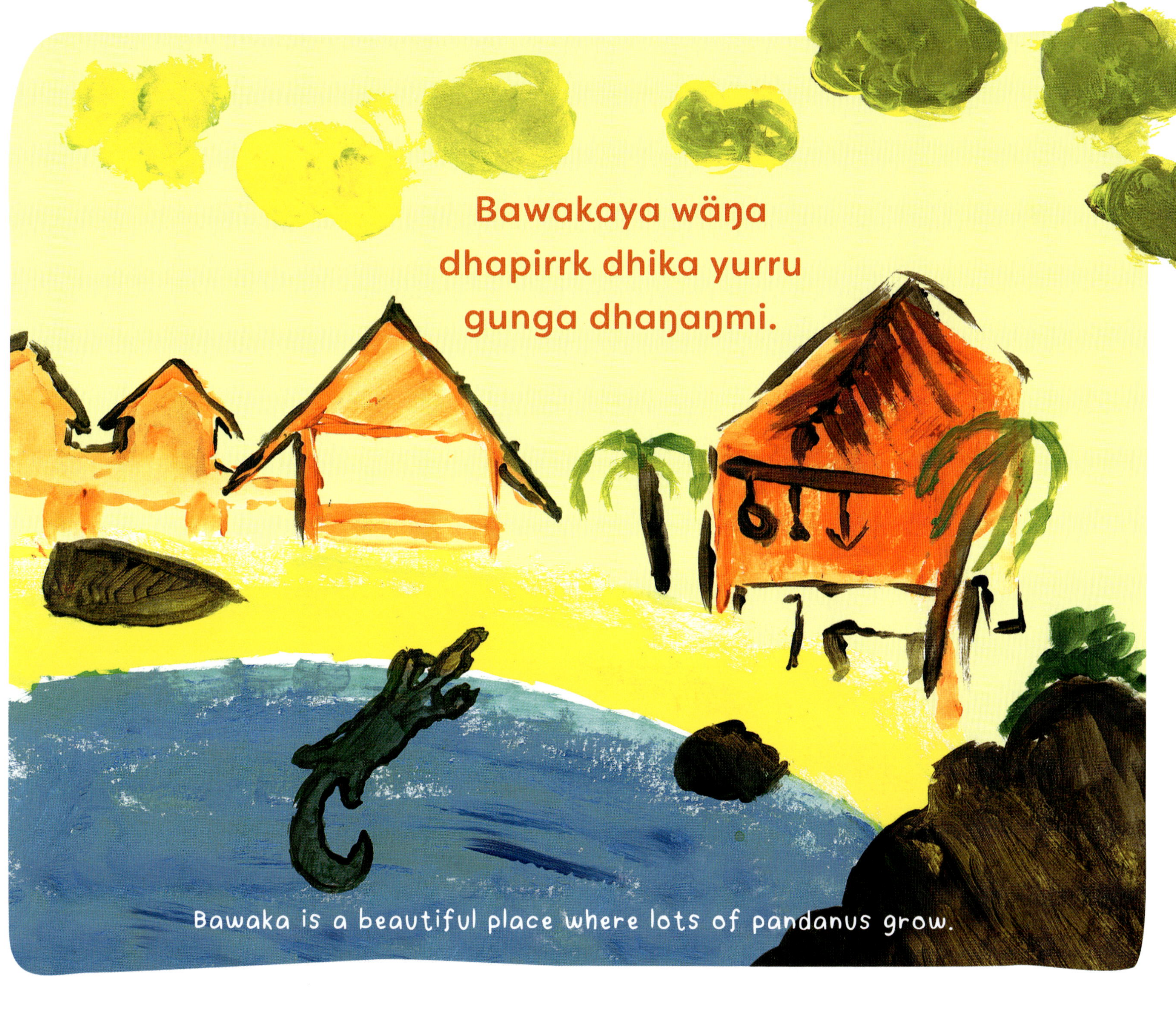

Bawakaya wäŋa dhapirrk dhika yurru gunga dhaŋaŋmi.

Bawaka is a beautiful place where lots of pandanus grow.

Galki wäŋaŋuya ŋanapuŋgaya bathala gul̲un' ga djunamayi man̲d̲a ŋunhi marrtjiya. Waŋanhamiya man̲d̲a marrtji ga gitkitthunmi. Dhuŋa ŋunhi man̲d̲a ŋayi gatapaŋaya galkun gurra retjaŋu. Man̲d̲aya birrkayun yana bini latju, gatapaŋamiriw wäŋa.

At the back of our house is a billabong and that's where they went. They were talking, laughing and giggling. They didn't know there was a big black beast waiting in the bushes. They thought it was safe.

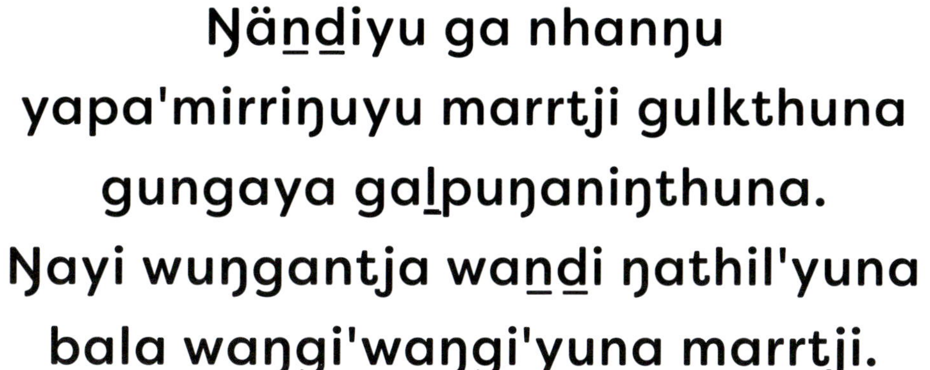

Ŋän̲d̲iyu ga nhanŋu
yapa'mirriŋuyu marrtji gulkthuna
gungaya gal̲puŋaniŋthuna.
Ŋayi wuŋgantja wan̲d̲i ŋathil'yuna
bala waŋgi'waŋgi'yuna marrtji.

Mum and Ruthie started collecting the pandanus,
using the tool to get it from the tree.

Roger the dog ran ahead, sniffing around.

Märr gurriri ma<u>n</u><u>d</u>a ŋäma wuŋgan'nha ŋayi gurra gukthun ŋula nhä. Ŋayi Ŋä<u>n</u><u>d</u>iya marrtji galkithina...bala nhäma...

After a while, they heard Roger barking at something. Mum went closer.

It was a ...

Gatapaŋa!
Yurru ŋayi wirrikina
ma<u>d</u>akarritjthi
wuŋganguna.

Buffalo!

And it was angry with Roger.

Yurru wanhakana nhanŋu yapamirriŋuya? Ŋän̲d̲iya marrtji l̲arrumana gawa'yun ŋayi, "Ruthie! Gatapaŋa dhuwa retjaŋu!"

But where was her sister?
Mum started panicking.
She called out, "Ruthie!
There's a buffalo in the bushes!"

Ruthie!

Wan̲d̲i man̲d̲a dharpayi.
Ŋayi ŋän̲d̲iya ŋurruŋuna ŋal'yun.
Ŋayi dhuwana räli gatapaŋaya galkithina.

They ran towards a tree.
Mum was first to climb.

Quick! The buffalo is coming!

Quick!

Ŋayi Ruthie-ya nhäma retja bala djoḻulyuna ŋunhimana.

Ruthie saw a bush nearby and hid herself amongst it.

Ŋän̲d̲iyuya ŋawatthun bilikan,
bala wutthuna rirrakayna djäma
märr ŋayi yurru gatapaŋayu ŋäma
ŋunhiyi rirrakay bala wan̲d̲ina.

D̲ar, d̲ar,
d̲ar, d̲ar!

Mum had a billy can and she hit it with a stick to make a noise to scare the buffalo away.

Bang! bang!
bang! bang!

Ŋän̲d̲i ga nhanŋu
yapamirriŋuya ŋäma
gatapaŋaya ŋayi wan̲d̲ina.

Mum and her sister could hear
the buffalo running away to
the other side of the road.

**Märr gurriri, man̲d̲a roŋiyi wäŋayina.
Bala ŋanapu nhenana bala dhäwuna
l̲akanhami ga gitkitthunmina ga
giyalamana gungaya.
Bilina.**

After a while, they both came back home.
And they sat with me, and they told me
the story, and we all laughed as we peeled
the pandanus together.